W9-DET-035

Rock Climbing

BY M. J. YORK

Published by The Child's World®
1980 Lookout Drive • Mankato, MN 56003-1705
800-599-READ • www.childsworld.com

Acknowledgments
The Child's World®: Mary Berendes, Publishing Director
Red Line Editorial: Editorial direction
The Design Lab: Design
Amnet: Production

Photographs ©: Shutterstock Images, cover (top), 1 (top), cover
(bottom), 1 (bottom), back cover (left), 3, 14, 20; Pavel L Photo
and Video/Shutterstock images, cover (center), 1 (center), 11;
Michele Caminati/Shutterstock Images, back cover (top), 14;
Thinkstock, back cover (right), 15, 18; Jupiter Images/Thinkstock,
4–5; Michael Thompson/Thinkstock, 7; Zoonar RF/Thinkstock,
8; Chris Rogers/Thinkstock, 9; Vergeles_Andrey/iStockphoto,
12; Yuriy Rudyy/Shutterstock Images, 16; Mariusz Szczygiel/
Shutterstock Images, 17; Igor Bulgarin/Shutterstock Images, 19;
John Audrey/Thinkstock, 21

ISBN 9781626873339
LCCN 2014930670

Printed in the United States of America
Mankato, MN
July, 2014
PA02222

ABOUT THE AUTHOR

M. J. York is a children's author and editor who lives in Minnesota. She has loved the outdoors her entire life and started camping, hiking, and canoeing at a young age.

CLIMBING HIGH

Do you like climbing? Maybe you climb trees. Or maybe you climb the jungle gym at the playground. Rock climbers **scale** boulders and cliffs. They even climb indoor climbing walls.

There are many reasons people enjoy rock climbing. Climbers enjoy being outside in

Rock climb to new heights!

CONTENTS

nature. They go in groups and use teamwork to reach their goals. They practice problem-solving skills to find their **routes**. Climbing is good exercise, too! Rock climbing can be a thrilling adventure.

WHAT IS ROCK CLIMBING?

Rock climbing is the sport of climbing steep mountains or cliffs. Some people practice climbing on indoor climbing walls in gyms. Some climbers use ropes or equipment in their **ascent**. Some use ropes only to catch them if they fall. And some use no ropes at all!

People have climbed mountains and cliffs for thousands of years. Most were traveling or looking for shelter. People began climbing mountains for fun in the 1700s. To scale mountaintops, adventurers had to work out better and safer ways to climb.

ANCIENT CLIMBERS

The ancient Pueblo people of the U.S. Southwest were expert climbers. They built their homes into cliff faces. Their biggest towns had hundreds of people. People used ladders to climb up or down the cliff to get home!

Today, some people try to reach the tops of mountains. But people don't have to scale mountains to enjoy rock climbing. Large rocks, cliffs, and mountainsides everywhere invite people to climb them, too.

The Pueblo people built their shelters into cliffs.

WHERE DO PEOPLE CLIMB?

Some people learn to climb indoors. Many gyms have climbing walls. A climbing wall has handholds and footholds. Some are more challenging to climb than others. Climbers use safety ropes. Trainers teach people how to climb. They also teach climbers how to stay safe.

Many people love to climb outdoors. Some climb over boulders. Others scale cliff walls. There is a climb for every skill level. The United States and other countries

RAPPELLING

Once a climber reaches the top, he or she usually has to get back down. One method is **rappelling** or abseiling. Rappelling is controlled sliding down a rope. The rope is **anchored** to a rock. Rappellers put their hands on the rope and their feet on the rock face. This helps them control the **descent**.

Ropes help keep a climber safe on a climbing wall or rock face.

have rating systems for climbing routes. These ratings tell climbers how difficult a route is to climb. These systems help climbers choose the right routes for them.

Many areas have climbing clubs. These groups get climbers together. The groups plan club trips. Club members learn from each other. Joining a climbing club is a great way to learn more about rock climbing.

CLIMBING STYLES

There are many types of rock climbing. Most modern climbers practice some kind of free climbing. Free climbers use only the power of their arms and legs to climb. They put their weight on the rock, not on ropes. But they use ropes and other gear to keep them safe from falls.

There are several types of free climbing. In top-rope climbing, the climber's safety rope is anchored at the top of the climb. Both traditional and sport climbing use anchors in the rock. Free climbers work with a partner called a **belayer**. The belayer holds the safety

ASSISTED CLIMBING

Assisted climbing or aid climbing uses gear similar to that used in free climbing. But unlike free climbing, assisted climbers sometimes put their weight on ropes or gear. Assisted climbing uses many anchors. This can damage the rock. People today do not often climb this way.

rope. He or she keeps the rope tight so the climber stays safe.

Some climbers do not use ropes. Bouldering is climbing big rocks or the base of cliffs. Climbers have a crash pad and a person **spotting** them for safety. They do not climb very high. This makes bouldering less dangerous. Solo climbing or soloing is for experts only. They climb high without ropes. It can be very dangerous if they fall.

This climber is using ropes to stay safe.

CLIMBING GEAR

Climbers use several pieces of equipment to stay safe. Ropes can save a climber's life in a fall. One type attaches the climber to the

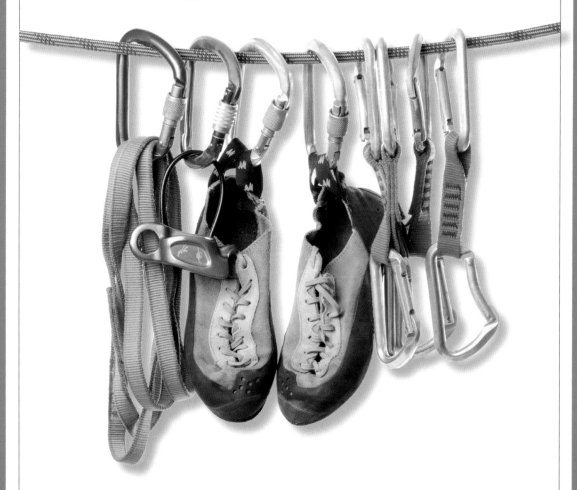

Climbing gear includes harnesses, shoes, and carabiners.

belayer. This rope has a little stretch. Ropes without stretch are used to attach equipment. They are also used for rappelling.

Anchors attach ropes to the rock. There are several types of anchors. Nuts, cams, chocks, and stops all fit into cracks in the rock. Some have springs so they expand to fit perfectly. Pitons are spikes hammered into the rock. This can damage the rock. That's why they are not often used anymore.

Both the climber and the belayer wear harnesses. Harnesses connect people to their ropes. There are harnesses for different types of climbs. Carabiners are metal loops with gates that open and close. They connect ropes to people's harnesses or to anchors in the rock. Climbers need to make sure a carabiner's gate is closed when in use.

SAFETY EQUIPMENT

The most important thing a climber wears is a helmet. A helmet can save a person's life in a fall. No one should ever climb without a helmet. A helmet needs to fit comfortably. It should not slide around on the climber's head. Climbers should always wear special climbing helmets. Bicycle or other helmets do not protect enough in a fall.

Climbers can buy shoes just for climbing. These have thin, **flexible** soles. They let climbers feel the rock with their feet. The soles are sticky rubber so the climber does not slip.

Climbing shoes and helmets help keep climbers safe.

Outdoor climbers need to dress for the weather. All climbers should wear comfortable clothes. Stretchy clothes allow arms and legs to move easily. Some materials even help keep a sweating climber dry.

CLIMBING CHALK
Sweaty or wet hands can make climbing tricky. Some climbers use chalk to keep their hands dry. It improves their grip on the rock. Chalk can be a block, powder, or liquid. Climbers keep their chalk in chalk bags.

Climbing chalk gives climbers a better grip.

CLIMBING SAFETY

Rock climbing can be dangerous. Using the right equipment and proper **technique** makes it safer. New climbers can take classes or join clubs. They can learn the skills they need from experts. Many new climbers

Indoor gyms are good places for beginner and expert climbers to practice.

practice at indoor climbing gyms. Experienced climbers learn advanced skills at climbing gyms, too.

Being fit helps climbers stay safe. People must be strong to climb difficult routes. Climbers exercise to get stronger. Strong arms and hands are very important. Being flexible is important, too. Flexible climbers can reach difficult handholds more easily. Climbers should stretch all their muscles often to stay flexible.

CLIMBING SKILLS

Some skills that help rock climbers stay safe include:

- knot tying
- placing anchors
- belaying
- balancing, changing handholds and footholds, and other climbing techniques
- rappelling and getting back down

Learning to tie knots is one simple way to help you stay safe while climbing.

PLANNING A CLIMB

Careful planning makes climbing trips safer. People should not climb alone. New climbers should choose climbs that are not too difficult.

Gear needs to be checked for safety before every climb. A checklist helps climbers keep track of the equipment they need. The checklist helps for packing. Climbers also use it as they're putting on gear for the climb. Climbers should check the five Hs before they climb:

- Harness is on correctly
- Helmet is on correctly
- Hardware is secure, including knots and carabiners
- Hair is out of the way
- The Human climber is ready to go

Check that your carabiners are secure before climbing.

Climbers should write out a plan for their trips. They should think about things that might go wrong. Their plan should tell them what to do if bad things happen. The plan should say when they're leaving. It should include when they will get back, too. Climbers should leave their plans with someone who is not climbing with them. This person can get help in case something goes wrong.

Leave a plan with someone before you wave good-bye and begin your rock climbing adventure.

REACHING NEW HEIGHTS

Climbing is exciting and adventurous. Climbers build teamwork skills. They learn to trust themselves and their teams. And they learn to get past **obstacles**. Climbing is a great way to get active, too!

LEAVE NO TRACE

Climbers should take care to leave no trace of their climbs. They should place anchors carefully. They should take home all their gear and garbage. They should not **disturb** nature or remove plants in their way.

Rock climbing is an adventurous way to get outside and enjoy nature. The views from up high are stunning. Climbing is a time to think. Climbers listen to the wind and to nature all around them. They get in tune with the rock and themselves.

Climbing is a challenging and exciting outdoor activity.

GLOSSARY

anchored (ANG-kurd): If something is anchored it is fixed in place. Ropes can be anchored to rock.

ascent (ah-SENT): An ascent is a climb. Climbers train for a difficult ascent.

belayer (bee-LAY-ur): A belayer is a climbing teammate who holds the safety rope. A belayer makes climbing safer.

descent (dee-SENT): A descent is coming down. A climber must plan his or her descent.

disturb (di-STURB): To disturb is to change or mess up something. Be careful not to disturb nature.

flexible (FLEK-suh-bul): Something flexible is able to bend or stretch. Climbers need to be strong and flexible.

obstacles (AHB-stuh-kuls): Obstacles are things that are in the way. Rocks and fallen trees are obstacles for climbers.

rappelling (ra-PEL-ing): Rappelling is a way to get down using ropes. Climbers practice their rappelling skills.

routes (roots) or (rowts): Routes are courses or paths. Climbers should plan their routes ahead of time.

scale (skale): To scale is to climb. Some climbers want to scale mountains.

spotting (SPAHT-ting): Spotting is watching a climber from below to help them to the ground safely if they start falling. Having someone spotting makes short climbs safer.

technique (tek-NEEK): Technique is a way of doing something that needs skill. Climbers should practice proper technique.

TO LEARN MORE

BOOKS

Champion, Neil. *Rock Climbing.* New York: PowerKids Press, 2010.

National Geographic Kids National Parks Guide USA: The Most Amazing Sights, Scenes, and Cool Activities from Coast to Coast. Washington, DC: National Geographic, 2012.

Weingarten, A. J. *Rock Climbing.* New York: Gareth Stevens Publishing, 2013.

WEB SITES

Visit our Web site for links about rock climbing:
childsworld.com/links

Note to Parents, Teachers, and Librarians: We routinely verify our Web links to make sure they are safe and active sites. So encourage your readers to check them out!

INDEX